For Mum, Dad & C.....
Thank you for everything

Copyright © 2024 by Lucy Butler
All rights reserved

No part of this book can be reproduced or used in any matter without the written permission of the author.

First edition August 2024

ISBN : 9798335726108

Independently Published

Lucy Butler's

HUGO THE DANCING HIPPO

Once in a jungle...

But was scared to show others.

The monkey said,
"You're just too
big to dance!"

And the lion said,
"Hippo's can't dance!"

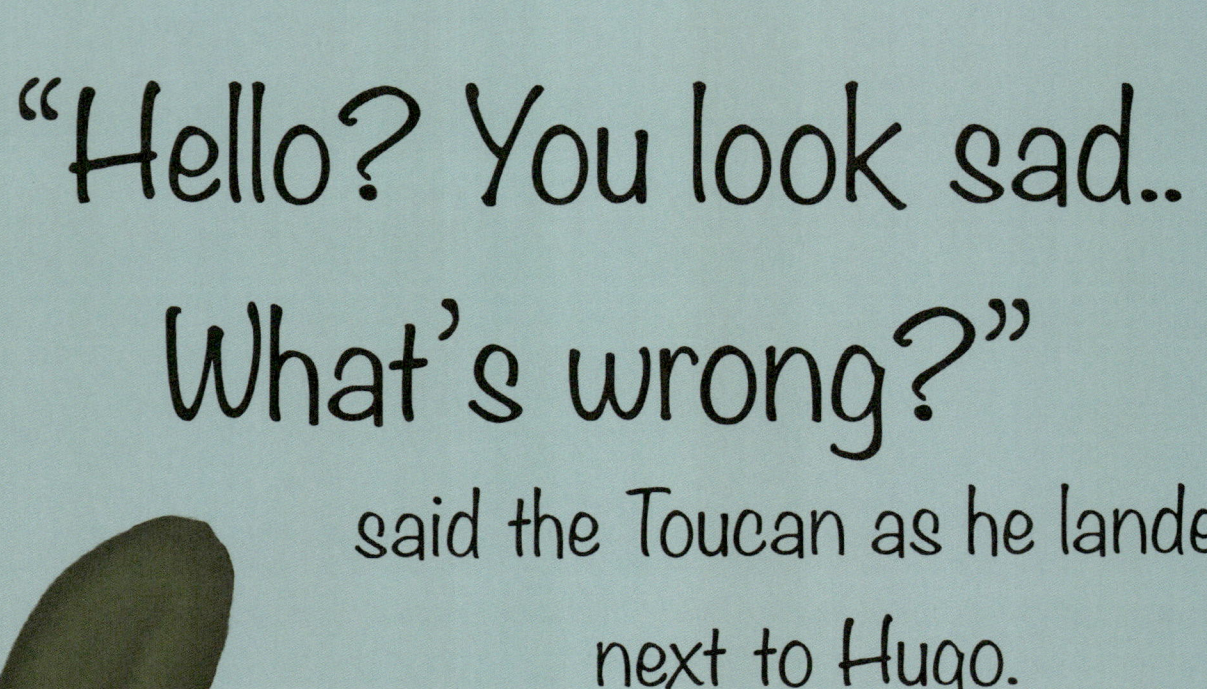

"Hello? You look sad..
What's wrong?"
said the Toucan as he landed next to Hugo.

The toucan told Hugo

"Dancing is about having fun and being yourself"

"It doesn't matter what others think!"

"Just take a breath, and go at your own speed"

And sometimes he fell...

One day, the lions and giraffes saw Hugo dancing and smiled!

The animals felt bad for being mean to Hugo, and let him join in with their show!

Hugo was so nervous!

But remembered what the Toucan told him...

So Hugo took 3 deep breaths.

Once Hugo finished dancing ... it was silent... until...

the animals celebrated! They loved Hugo's dancing!

YAY
Woo
Woo
YAY
YAY
Woo

Printed in Great Britain
by Amazon